Mist
THE SHEEPDOG

Mist
THE SHEEPDOG
Nicky Daw

Photographs by Liz Bomford

Hippo Books
Scholastic Publications Limited
London

Scholastic Publications Ltd.,
10 Earlham Street, London WC2H 9RX, UK

Scholastic Inc.,
730 Broadway, New York, NY 10003, USA

Scholastic Tab Publications Ltd.,
123 Newkirk Road, Richmond Hill,
Ontario, L4C 3G5, Canada

Ashton Scholastic Pty. Ltd.,
P O Box 579, Gosford, New South Wales,
Australia

Ashton Scholastic Ltd.,
165 Marua Road, Panmure, Auckland 6,
New Zealand

First published by A & C Black (Publishers) Limited, UK, 1986
under the title *Sheepdog*

Published in paperback by Scholastic Publications Ltd., UK, 1988

The author and publishers would like to thank George Bates
for making this book possible.

ISBN 0 590 70791 4

Made and printed by Everbest, Hong Kong

Other titles available
in this series:
Pang Pon The Elephant
Danny The Guide Dog
Lloyd The Police Horse

George is a shepherd. He looks after a flock of five hundred sheep.

It is very difficult for George to move his sheep from one place to another, especially on the mountains around his farm. Sheep won't go where you tell them. So George trains sheepdogs to help him round up all his sheep.

2

This is Mist. She is the young Welsh border collie that George is training at the moment.

Mist was born on George's farm. Here she is with her mother and her brothers and sisters.

While Mist is still a puppy, George takes her to look at a small flock of sheep. George keeps these sheep in a little field especially for training his dogs. George takes Mist to the field once a week so that she gets used to the sheep and isn't frightened of them.

Even at this age Mist wants to round up the hens!

Mist is six months old and she has started to be very interested in the sheep. Now she is ready for training.

Mist lives in a little shed that is dry and clean. George looks after her very carefully and gives her plenty of food. Mist is strong and healthy. She will want to please George because he looks after her so well.

George is about to take Mist for her first training session. One of George's other dogs wishes that she could come too.

George's sheep are used to being rounded up, but they can tell that a new young dog is coming into their field. They don't look too pleased.

Collie dogs have been working with sheep for hundreds of years. You don't have to teach a young collie to round up sheep. It does this because of its 'instinct'. In just the same way, a kitten is born with the instinct to chase mice.

George has to teach Mist to take the sheep where he wants, not where she wants as she's doing here.

At first, Mist is so excited that she just chases the sheep into a huddle. George says her name loudly over and over again. He wants to remind her that he is the boss.

When Mist hears her name, she begins to calm down. The sheep know that Mist means business!

10

The three most important commands that Mist
has to learn are 'Right', 'Left' and 'Stop'.
George lets Mist go on rounding up the sheep.
When she runs out to her left, George shouts
'Away Mist!'

George says this again and again. In the end,
Mist will know that 'Away' means she must move
to her left. The command 'Come by' means she
should go to the right and the command 'Stand'
means she should stop.

It will take many training sessions for Mist to learn the commands properly. At first, George has to do a lot of running about to help teach Mist. He uses his stick to point with, and to help Mist round up the sheep.

The way George says
'Mist!' is very important.
If she is doing something
wrong, George will say
'Mist!' in a stern voice.
George never hits his dogs.

Here he is scolding Mist
because she has run into
the middle of the flock of
sheep. He takes hold of
the hair on her neck and
gives her a little shake.
It doesn't hurt her but
she knows she mustn't
do that again!

Mist is doing well and George says 'Good dog, Mist!' After about twenty minutes of training, George thinks Mist is getting tired. He calls her over to him, pats her and gives her lots of praise.

Mist's first training sessions have gone very well. From now on George will give her a short lesson every evening.

When Mist is older she will help George to round up sheep on the mountain and she might go too far away to hear his voice. So George teaches her a different whistle for each command. George's whistle is very loud and piercing and Mist can hear it from far away.

Mist has to stop training for a week because she
is ill. George's sheepdogs never go into the
farmhouse but, because Mist must be kept warm,
George puts a special heat-lamp in her shed.
He makes a big fuss of her. Soon she is better
and ready for more training.

Mist isn't so excitable now. She moves more carefully, always listening for George's whistle which will tell her where to go next.

When George gives the command, Mist will creep softly behind the sheep to make them move very slowly. She couldn't have done this two months ago.

Mist will move to the right and to the left whenever George tells her to. She will stand or come to George. Here, she is taking the sheep away up to the corner of the field. George doesn't need to run around with Mist any more. He can have a rest.

Although Mist is learning fast it will be quite a long time before she can do really difficult jobs for George.

This is Nell, one of the older dogs. George wants to look at one of his rams. He sends Nell into the flock. Because George gives the right whistles, Nell brings the ram out towards him.

But this ram is an awkward customer. He doesn't want to be rounded up at all. He and Nell look at each other. Who will give in?

The ram is much bigger than Nell. But Nell is so well trained that her eyes never move from the ram, even when he charges her. In the end, he gives in. One day Mist will be able to work with rams, too.

Every summer George takes his best dogs to the Sheepdog Trials. These are competitions to see how well each sheepdog has been trained. George decides to take Mist along too, just to watch and to get used to seeing other people.

When they arrive George gives the dogs a drink. They are very excited.

At the Trials, each shepherd has to make his dog bring four sheep down a large field and into a little pen. This is very difficult.

Mist cannot take her eyes off the sheep. George and Mist watch George's friend, Mike. It takes him and his dog quite a long time to get the four sheep into the pen.

When it is George's turn he goes into the field with Nell. She manages to drive the sheep into the pen quite quickly. At the end of the morning the judges add up the marks. George and Nell have won the cup!

For Mist, this is the boring part of the Trials. Now that there are no sheep to look at, she wants to go home.

This time next year she will be working with George out on the mountain. And, who knows? She and George might even win that cup at the Sheep Dog Trials!

More about sheepdogs

Sheepdogs have played an important part in sheep-farming for thousands of years and in many countries.

For generations, border collies, like Mist, have been specially bred to work and a young collie will round up by instinct. All good dogs are registered so that anyone buying a puppy can study its breeding; but even a well bred collie will not work properly unless it is carefully trained. A shepherd will only start training when he thinks the dog is ready. Many dogs start their training at about six months and can work to commands by the time they are twelve months old.

Working collies always have short names, such as Nell, Bess, Fly or Mist; their names must be easy to say when the shepherd is giving quick commands. A shepherd with a large flock of sheep might use several dogs at once, so each dog must answer to its own name. Most shepherds use spoken and whistled commands. There are five basic commands: 'Go right', 'Go left', 'Stop', 'Come on' and 'Come here'. Many shepherds use the same commands. This makes it easier to sell or exchange the dogs.

Sheepdog Trials test a shepherd's skill in training a dog. People who want to buy a puppy can see its relations working. Other people just enjoy watching a shepherd and a dog working as a team.

Index

This index will help you to find some of the important words in the book.

collie 3, 9 25
commands 11, 12, 15, 18, 25
creeping 18

eyes 21, 23

flock 2, 5, 13, 20, 25
food 6

heat-lamp 16
hens 5
huddle 10

ill 16
instinct 9, 25

mountains 2, 15, 24

Nell 20, 21, 24

pen 23, 24
praise 14
puppy 4, 5, 25

ram 20, 21
round up 2, 5, 8, 9, 11, 12, 15, 21, 25

scolding 13
shed 6, 16
sheep 2, 5, 6, 7, 8, 9, 10, 11, 12, 15, 18, 23, 24, 25
Sheepdog Trials 22, 23, 24, 25
shepherd 2, 23, 25

voice 13, 15

whistle 15, 17, 20, 25